Legacy of Luxury
The Rise of Alexandre Arnault

From Inheritance to Innovation
Shaping the Future of the World's
Most Iconic Brands

Beatrice G. George

Copyright © Beatrice G. George 2024

No part of this publication may be reproduced, distributed, or transmitted in any form or by any means, including photocopying, recording, or other electronic or mechanical methods, without the prior written permission of the publisher, except in the case of brief quotations embodied in critical reviews and certain other noncommercial uses permitted by copyright law.

Table Of Contents

Introduction

Chapter 1: Early Life and Education
Formative Influences
Preparation for the Future

Chapter 2: Career Path
Role at Rimowa
Transition to Tiffany & Co.
Defining Leadership Style

Chapter 3: Impact at Tiffany & Co.
Brand Modernization and Visual Identity
Rebuilding Tiffany's Global Reputation
Legacy and Future Prospects

Chapter 4: Personal Experiences
High-Profile Wedding and Social Connections
Balancing Work and Personal Life

Chapter 5: Legacy
Shaping the Future of Luxury

Chapter 6: Net Worth
Influence of Family Wealth
Financial Independence and Personal Investments

Conclusion

Introduction

Born into a family synonymous with opulence and innovation, Alexandre Arnault has emerged as a key architect of modern luxury. On May 5, 1992, in Neuilly-sur-Seine, France, Alexandre was welcomed into the world as the son of Bernard Arnault, the chairman of LVMH, the world's largest luxury conglomerate. His story, however, is not merely one of inheritance but of a determined ascent marked by strategy, creativity, and relentless ambition.

Today, Alexandre Arnault stands as the Executive Vice President of Tiffany & Co., a position that places him at the forefront of redefining one of the globe's most iconic jewelry brands. From an early age, Alexandre's life was steeped in the culture of excellence and refinement that defines LVMH's portfolio. The family name carried both immense privilege and an unspoken expectation of brilliance, and Alexandre rose to meet this challenge with a mix of discipline and innovation. While the world often focuses on the allure of luxury goods, Alexandre's journey reveals the rigorous business acumen and forward-thinking mindset that drives the industry's success.

His early years in France were shaped by an environment where the lines between personal and professional often blurred. Being raised in one of Europe's most influential families meant frequent exposure to high-level discussions about brand strategy, market dynamics, and innovation. Yet, Alexandre's upbringing wasn't simply about luxury; it was rooted in a strong emphasis on hard work and earning one's achievements.

This duality—balancing inherited privilege with personal merit—has defined his approach to life and work. Education played a pivotal role in shaping Alexandre's trajectory. He attended Lycée Louis-le-Grand, one of France's most prestigious secondary schools, known for fostering critical thinking and intellectual rigor. This foundation prepared him for his studies at École Polytechnique, where he earned a master's degree in innovation. These formative years honed his ability to combine technical expertise with creative vision, a combination that would later become central to his career. While many might assume a direct and predictable path to the helm of an LVMH brand, Alexandre's journey was anything but conventional.

Before diving into the family business, he carved out a professional identity at globally recognized firms like McKinsey & Company and KKR in New York. These experiences outside the family's immediate sphere allowed him to develop his analytical and strategic skills, making him well-equipped for the challenges of leading in the competitive world of luxury retail. In 2015, Alexandre took a decisive step toward the family business when he joined LVMH as an Investment Manager.

His early impact was felt at Rimowa, where he became CEO at just 24 years old. Under his leadership, Rimowa transformed from a traditional luggage brand into a symbol of contemporary luxury. Alexandre's innovative approach brought collaborations with trend-setting partners like Supreme and Off-White, elevating Rimowa into a cultural icon. This success demonstrated his ability to modernize heritage brands while preserving their core identity, a skill that would later prove invaluable at Tiffany & Co. In 2021, LVMH acquired Tiffany & Co., a $15.8 billion deal that marked a milestone for the conglomerate. Alexandre was entrusted with a pivotal role at Tiffany, overseeing its transition into a new era.

His efforts to revitalize the brand included bold marketing campaigns, fresh product designs, and collaborations with global icons such as Beyoncé and Jay-Z. These initiatives showcased Alexandre's knack for balancing tradition with innovation, ensuring Tiffany remained relevant to both loyal customers and a younger, more diverse audience. But Alexandre's story extends beyond boardrooms and branding strategies. His personal life, too, reflects a blend of legacy and individuality.

In 2021, he married Géraldine Guyot in a celebrated wedding that underscored his social and cultural connections. Beyond his professional achievements, Alexandre is also known for his creative pursuits, particularly his passion for music as a DJ. This personal dimension adds depth to his persona, revealing a man who thrives not only on business success but also on artistic expression and cultural engagement. As the luxury industry evolves, Alexandre Arnault is poised to play a defining role in shaping its future. His journey so far has been a testament to the power of combining inherited opportunities with personal drive and innovation.

More than a scion of one of the world's most powerful families, Alexandre is carving out a legacy of his own—one that could very well see him ascend to the pinnacle of the LVMH empire. In this biography, we will delve into the facets of Alexandre's life, from his formative years and career milestones to his personal passions and enduring impact on the luxury sector. By examining his journey, we gain insight into the delicate balance between tradition and transformation, privilege and effort, and the enduring allure of innovation in a rapidly changing world.

Chapter 1: Early Life and Education

Alexandre Arnault's origins are rooted in a legacy of vision and excellence. Born into one of Europe's wealthiest and most influential families, Alexandre was the third child of Bernard Arnault, the mastermind behind LVMH (Moët Hennessy Louis Vuitton), and his second wife, Hélène Mercier, a renowned Canadian pianist. This family dynamic placed Alexandre at the intersection of two distinct worlds: the corporate brilliance of his father and the artistic refinement of his mother.

Growing up in Neuilly-sur-Seine, a suburb of Paris synonymous with affluence, Alexandre was surrounded by privilege but also by high expectations. Bernard Arnault's empire wasn't merely about amassing wealth but about leading the luxury industry with creativity and innovation. This ethos permeated the Arnault household, where children were encouraged to dream big but also to work hard. Alexandre's formative years were marked by exposure to the luxury business. Whether accompanying his father on visits to LVMH's vast portfolio of brands or observing discussions about market strategies at home, he absorbed the language of the industry.

Yet, Bernard Arnault instilled in his children a strong sense of humility, emphasizing that privilege came with responsibility. From a young age, Alexandre exhibited an intellectual curiosity and drive for excellence. He was enrolled in Lycée Louis-le-Grand, one of France's most prestigious secondary schools, known for producing leaders in various fields. The school's rigorous academic environment honed his analytical abilities and fostered a passion for problem-solving.

After excelling at Lycée Louis-le-Grand, Alexandre pursued higher education at École Polytechnique, another elite institution in France. At École Polytechnique, he earned a master's degree in Innovation, a field that perfectly aligned with his aspirations. The program equipped him with a deep understanding of technology, design, and business strategy—skills that would later define his approach to leadership. École Polytechnique also exposed Alexandre to a diverse group of peers and mentors, broadening his perspective and sharpening his ability to collaborate with individuals from various backgrounds. This experience was pivotal in shaping his vision for blending tradition and innovation in the luxury sector.

Beyond academics, Alexandre's educational journey reflected his capacity to balance multiple interests. While excelling in his studies, he also explored creative outlets, including his passion for music. This multidimensional approach to life would later become one of his defining characteristics.

Formative Influences

Alexandre's education wasn't confined to classrooms and textbooks. The Arnault family placed a strong emphasis on experiential learning, often involving their children in cultural and business-related activities. These experiences cultivated a global perspective and an appreciation for the finer details that define luxury. One of the key lessons Alexandre learned from his father was the importance of long-term vision. Bernard Arnault often spoke about building brands that could stand the test of time, emphasizing quality, craftsmanship, and innovation. These principles resonated with Alexandre, who began to view the luxury industry not just as a business but as an art form.

Additionally, his mother's musical career exposed him to the world of performance and aesthetics. Watching her bring compositions to life instilled in Alexandre a deep respect for creativity and discipline—qualities he would later channel into his professional endeavors. While Alexandre's background offered unparalleled opportunities, it also came with its challenges.

The expectations placed on him as the son of Bernard Arnault were immense, and living up to the family name required more than inherited privilege. Alexandre faced these pressures with a blend of determination and humility, striving to carve out his own identity within the luxury industry. His time at École Polytechnique was particularly formative in this regard. The rigorous curriculum tested his resilience, while the collaborative environment helped him develop the interpersonal skills necessary for leadership. These experiences laid the groundwork for his future successes, proving that Alexandre was more than just the heir to a dynasty—he was a capable and innovative thinker in his own right.

Preparation for the Future

By the time Alexandre completed his education, he had amassed a wealth of knowledge and experiences that positioned him for a prominent role in the luxury sector. His academic achievements, combined with the values instilled by his family, set the stage for a career defined by innovation, strategy, and a deep respect for tradition.

The next chapter of Alexandre's life would see him stepping into the professional world, where he would apply the lessons of his upbringing and education to make a lasting impact. From the classrooms of France's most prestigious institutions to the boardrooms of LVMH, Alexandre's journey was just beginning. This chapter captures the foundation of Alexandre Arnault's story, highlighting the unique blend of privilege, discipline, and ambition that has shaped his path. It is a testament to the power of education, both formal and experiential, in preparing individuals for greatness.

Chapter 2: Career Path

After completing his education, Alexandre Arnault began laying the groundwork for what would become an impressive career. Unlike many heirs to business empires, he sought to establish his own credibility and prove his merit in the professional world. His journey began at McKinsey & Company, one of the world's leading management consulting firms, where he gained exposure to strategic problem-solving and operational efficiency across various industries.

At McKinsey, Alexandre developed critical skills in analysis, decision-making, and leadership. Working alongside some of the brightest minds, he honed his ability to think both analytically and creatively—traits essential for his eventual role in the luxury sector. Following his tenure at McKinsey, Alexandre joined the global investment firm KKR in New York, diving into the world of private equity. This experience provided him with a deeper understanding of corporate finance and investment strategies, particularly in high-stakes environments. It also marked his first professional foray outside of France, giving him valuable international exposure.

Role at Rimowa

In 2015, Alexandre transitioned to LVMH, taking on the role of Investment Manager. It wasn't long before he was entrusted with a more significant leadership opportunity. At just 24 years old, he was appointed CEO of Rimowa, the German luxury luggage brand acquired by LVMH in the same year. This appointment was a bold move, demonstrating Bernard Arnault's confidence in his son's abilities.

At Rimowa, Alexandre spearheaded a transformation that would redefine the brand. Prior to his leadership, Rimowa was known primarily for its high-quality aluminum suitcases. Alexandre saw the potential to modernize its image and appeal to a younger, style-conscious audience. He introduced strategic collaborations with renowned brands and designers, such as Supreme, Off-White, and Fendi, which elevated Rimowa's status from a functional luggage maker to a coveted fashion statement. These partnerships not only showcased Alexandre's innovative thinking but also underscored his understanding of contemporary consumer trends.

Under his leadership, Rimowa embraced digital transformation, including the launch of an e-commerce platform and a robust presence on social media. These initiatives expanded the brand's reach and modernized its marketing approach. By blending traditional craftsmanship with cutting-edge design and technology, Alexandre positioned Rimowa as a leader in the luxury travel sector.

Transition to Tiffany & Co.

In 2021, following LVMH's acquisition of Tiffany & Co. for $15.8 billion, Alexandre was appointed Executive Vice President for Product and Communications. This marked a significant step in his career, as Tiffany & Co. was one of the most high-profile acquisitions in LVMH's history. Alexandre faced the formidable challenge of revitalizing an iconic but somewhat stagnant brand. His approach was rooted in preserving Tiffany's heritage while infusing it with a fresh, contemporary appeal. This included modernizing its product lines, introducing bold marketing campaigns, and reimagining its flagship stores to create immersive retail experiences.

At Tiffany, Alexandre's contributions were transformative. One of his standout strategies was redefining the brand's visual identity. This included a fresh take on Tiffany's signature shade of blue and introducing a new slogan, "Not Your Mother's Tiffany." While controversial, this campaign succeeded in capturing public attention and positioning the brand as relevant to younger audiences.

Alexandre also oversaw collaborations with high-profile celebrities like Beyoncé and Jay-Z, whose partnership with Tiffany helped bridge the gap between luxury and pop culture. These initiatives signaled a bold departure from the brand's traditional marketing strategies, aligning Tiffany with a more diverse and dynamic audience. Furthermore, Alexandre prioritized sustainability, emphasizing responsible sourcing of materials like diamonds and gold. This commitment not only aligned with evolving consumer values but also reinforced Tiffany's legacy as a leader in ethical luxury.

Defining Leadership Style

Throughout his career, Alexandre has demonstrated a leadership style that blends analytical precision with creative vision. He is deeply involved in the details of product development, branding, and consumer engagement, often working closely with designers and marketing teams. His ability to balance tradition with innovation has been a recurring theme, enabling him to revitalize brands while maintaining their core identity.

Alexandre's journey through McKinsey, KKR, Rimowa, and Tiffany & Co. reflects a pattern of calculated risks and bold decisions. He has consistently sought opportunities to innovate and redefine traditional business models, emerging as a visionary leader in the luxury industry. This chapter illustrates not only Alexandre's professional achievements but also his ability to adapt and thrive in diverse roles. His career trajectory serves as a testament to his ambition, resilience, and commitment to excellence, laying the foundation for his growing influence within LVMH and the broader luxury sector.

Chapter 3: Impact at Tiffany & Co.

When LVMH acquired Tiffany & Co. in 2021 for a staggering $15.8 billion, it marked one of the largest-ever acquisitions in the luxury sector. Alexandre Arnault, appointed as Executive Vice President for Product and Communications, was tasked with a formidable challenge: to breathe new life into an iconic brand that had somewhat lost its relevance in the fast-changing luxury market.

Tiffany had long been associated with traditional elegance and exclusivity, but as consumer preferences shifted, its allure had started to fade among younger generations. Alexandre's vision for Tiffany was to keep the brand's rich heritage intact while modernizing its image to appeal to a more diverse, youthful audience. He believed that in order to attract a younger demographic, Tiffany needed to reframe its identity without sacrificing its core values. His strategy was clear: to merge tradition with innovation, luxury with accessibility, and exclusivity with inclusivity.

Brand Modernization and Visual Identity

One of Alexandre's first moves was to reimagine Tiffany's visual identity. The iconic Tiffany Blue, known worldwide for its elegance, was retained but given a fresh, modern twist. Alexandre introduced bold changes in branding, moving away from the more conservative image Tiffany had maintained for decades. This shift was most prominently seen in the 2021 launch of the "Not Your Mother's Tiffany" campaign, a provocative slogan that generated buzz across the fashion and luxury media.

The campaign aimed to redefine the brand as modern, inclusive, and progressive—qualities that were vital for attracting a younger, more diverse customer base. The campaign was controversial but successful. It signaled a decisive break from the past and positioned Tiffany as a brand that embraced change, resonating with younger consumers who valued authenticity and innovation in luxury products. Another cornerstone of Alexandre's strategy was leveraging celebrity collaborations to bring a fresh and edgy energy to Tiffany. One of the most significant moves was the partnership with Beyoncé and Jay-Z, two of the biggest global names in music and fashion.

The collaboration between the power couple and Tiffany marked a bold step for the luxury jewelry brand. Beyoncé's appearance in Tiffany's "About Love" campaign, where she wore the legendary Tiffany Diamond, created a media frenzy. This partnership not only brought attention to the brand but also connected Tiffany with pop culture in a way it never had before. By aligning Tiffany with high-profile celebrities, Alexandre successfully modernized the brand's image and showcased its relevance in the 21st-century luxury market.

But Beyoncé and Jay-Z weren't the only celebrities who would help Tiffany reach a new audience. Alexandre pushed for further collaborations with influencers, artists, and designers who embodied the youthful, creative spirit that Tiffany aimed to embrace. These partnerships helped to elevate Tiffany from a traditional, conservative luxury brand to one that was seen as forward-thinking and innovative. Under Alexandre's leadership, Tiffany's flagship stores also underwent significant transformations. One of the most notable changes was the redesign of the iconic Tiffany flagship store on Fifth Avenue in New York City. While the store still celebrated Tiffany's classic elegance, it now offered a more immersive and experiential retail experience.

Alexandre aimed to make the shopping experience more dynamic and engaging, appealing to a new generation of luxury shoppers who seek not just products but experiences. The new design incorporated modern art, creative showcases, and cutting-edge technology. It was no longer just a place to shop; it became a destination in itself. This move mirrored the trends in luxury retail where stores evolve into spaces where customers can engage, experience, and connect with the brand in meaningful ways.

In addition to physical spaces, Alexandre recognized the growing importance of digital engagement. Tiffany embraced e-commerce and social media to build stronger connections with younger consumers. The introduction of online shopping platforms, along with a more vibrant presence on social media channels like Instagram and TikTok, allowed Tiffany to reach a broader audience than ever before. With consumer consciousness increasingly centered on sustainability and ethical sourcing, Alexandre Arnault also made it a priority to ensure that Tiffany's products met the highest standards in these areas.

The brand made significant strides in sourcing diamonds and precious metals responsibly, aligning with the broader luxury industry's move toward more ethical practices. Tiffany also increased its transparency, providing consumers with detailed information about the origins of its materials and the steps it took to ensure fair labor practices and environmental responsibility. Alexandre understood that the luxury consumer of today wants not only to buy an exclusive product but also to feel good about the impact of their purchases.

By embracing sustainability, Alexandre not only catered to a socially conscious generation of consumers but also reinforced Tiffany's reputation as a leader in luxury. This commitment to responsible luxury helped the brand secure its place in the future, maintaining both its exclusivity and relevance in an ever-changing marketplace. Alongside these branding and marketing strategies, Alexandre was instrumental in reshaping Tiffany's product lines. While the brand's signature engagement rings, diamonds, and sterling silver pieces continued to perform well, Alexandre recognized the need for product diversification. Tiffany began releasing bolder designs, including more gender-neutral collections and pieces that pushed the boundaries of traditional jewelry design.

Collaborations with designers like Daniel Arsham, who brought a contemporary and artistic edge to the brand, added to Tiffany's appeal among a younger, more experimental audience. Additionally, Alexandre saw the potential for Tiffany to tap into new product categories. Limited-edition accessories, home goods, and luxury watches were introduced as part of the expanded product portfolio, furthering the brand's diversification while remaining true to its luxury roots.

Rebuilding Tiffany's Global Reputation

Perhaps the most notable achievement of Alexandre's time at Tiffany has been his ability to re-establish the brand's global reputation. Tiffany had, for many years, been the quintessential American luxury brand, a status it held thanks to its long history and iconic status in Hollywood and pop culture. However, in recent years, it had begun to lose some of its sparkle as competitors like Cartier and Bulgari gained market share. Alexandre's efforts to reimagine Tiffany allowed the brand to reassert its leadership in the luxury sector. By combining bold marketing strategies, high-profile collaborations, and a commitment to sustainability, Alexandre ensured that Tiffany remained a significant force in the competitive luxury market.

Legacy and Future Prospects

Alexandre Arnault's impact at Tiffany & Co. cannot be understated. In a relatively short period, he transformed the brand's image, product offerings, and global appeal. His focus on modernity, inclusivity, and sustainability allowed Tiffany to remain relevant and prosperous in the modern luxury marketplace. Moving forward, Alexandre's role at Tiffany will continue to evolve as the luxury sector changes. His understanding of digital marketing, customer engagement, and product innovation positions him to guide the brand into the future. As a potential successor to his father, Bernard Arnault, in LVMH's leadership, Alexandre's legacy at Tiffany will likely serve as a defining chapter in his broader career.

Chapter 4: Personal Experiences

Alexandre Arnault's upbringing in the Arnault family was one steeped in both privilege and responsibility. As the son of Bernard Arnault, the billionaire chairman and CEO of LVMH, Alexandre was exposed to the world of high luxury from an early age. However, despite the family's immense wealth, the values instilled in him were not centered solely around affluence but rather around hard work, discipline, and a sense of duty.

From a young age, Alexandre was taught that success is not a given but something that must be earned. His father, while being a key figure in Alexandre's life, emphasized the importance of personal achievement. Despite the enormous resources available to him, Alexandre never relied solely on his family name but rather worked diligently to carve his own path in the business world. This ethos was vital in shaping his character as he ventured into the corporate world, where his name might open doors, but his skills and determination would ultimately define his success. Alexandre's parents also taught him the importance of balancing ambition with personal integrity.

While Bernard Arnault is known for his relentless drive, he has also been known to prioritize family and long-term values over short-term gains. These principles were passed down to Alexandre, who continues to uphold them in both his personal and professional life.

High-Profile Wedding and Social Connections

In 2021, Alexandre Arnault married Géraldine Guyot, further solidifying his place within the elite circles of global business and culture. The wedding was a lavish affair that drew significant attention from both the fashion and celebrity worlds. Held at the exclusive Château de Versailles, the event was attended by a host of high-profile figures, ranging from business tycoons to Hollywood stars. Among the many notable guests were Kanye West, who performed at the wedding, and several prominent figures from the worlds of fashion, business, and entertainment. The wedding was seen not only as a union of two individuals but also as a fusion of two influential families in the world of luxury and business. Géraldine Guyot, an entrepreneur in her own right and founder of the jewelry brand "Rivecour," is known for her keen sense of style and innovation.

The couple's relationship is an embodiment of Alexandre's personal values—an individual whose professional success is matched by his commitment to family and meaningful relationships. The marriage also placed Alexandre and Géraldine firmly in the spotlight, as their combined influence in both the fashion and luxury industries brought even greater attention to their professional pursuits. Their social standing and wide-reaching networks have allowed them to strengthen ties with key figures in various industries, from the world of haute couture to entertainment and finance.

Alexandre's high-profile wedding exemplifies not only his personal milestones but also the social and professional capital that comes with his family's legacy. Beyond his professional endeavors, Alexandre Arnault has several personal interests and hobbies that further shape his character. One of his most well-known passions is music, specifically DJing. Alexandre has been an avid fan of electronic music for many years and has occasionally performed at private events and parties. His love for music offers a creative outlet and provides a contrast to his corporate work, allowing him to express himself in a different medium. DJing, for Alexandre, is more than just a hobby—it's a form of artistic expression.

It's also a way for him to connect with a younger, more diverse audience, as his performances often take place in more informal and avant-garde settings. His involvement in the music scene reflects his belief in embracing a variety of creative outlets, which also influences his approach to branding and product design in his professional life. This passion for music ties into his broader worldview of blending culture, creativity, and business, traits that have also been essential in shaping his approach to revitalizing Tiffany & Co.

In addition to music, Alexandre is also passionate about technology, particularly innovation and digital transformation. This interest is reflected in his work at LVMH, where he has pushed for the integration of digital tools in luxury retail. His understanding of the growing importance of e-commerce, social media, and digital marketing in the luxury sector has been pivotal in his efforts to modernize Tiffany. This passion for technology is not only a professional asset but also a personal interest that keeps him on the cutting edge of both the business and cultural worlds. Alexandre also values fitness and well-being, often sharing glimpses of his athletic routines and active lifestyle on social media.

Whether it's hiking, running, or training in the gym, his dedication to physical health reflects a disciplined approach to all areas of his life. Despite his prominent role in the luxury world, Alexandre Arnault is not immune to the broader social and environmental concerns of the modern age. As the luxury industry becomes increasingly scrutinized for its environmental and ethical practices, Alexandre has shown a commitment to improving sustainability and social responsibility within his brands.

At Tiffany & Co., for instance, Alexandre has helped prioritize ethical sourcing of materials, including sustainable mining practices for diamonds and precious metals. This focus on sustainability is not just a business strategy but also a reflection of Alexandre's own values. He has spoken publicly about the importance of responsible luxury, emphasizing that the future of high-end brands lies in their ability to balance quality with environmental stewardship. Additionally, Alexandre has been involved in various charitable initiatives. While he tends to maintain a low profile when it comes to his philanthropic activities, he has supported causes related to education, arts, and the environment.

His family's legacy of philanthropy, led by Bernard Arnault's own charitable work, has had a significant influence on his own approach to giving back. Alexandre believes that business success should translate into positive societal impact, a principle that guides both his personal and professional decisions.

Balancing Work and Personal Life

While Alexandre's career in the luxury sector is demanding, he places a high value on maintaining a balanced life. His ability to juggle the intense pressures of running major luxury brands with his personal life is a testament to his disciplined and focused approach. Alexandre has often spoken about the importance of having a clear sense of priorities and managing his time effectively. His commitment to his family, friends, and personal interests ensures that he remains grounded, even as he navigates the high-stakes world of international business. His approach to work-life balance also influences his leadership style. Alexandre understands the importance of fostering a positive work culture that values not only productivity but also well-being.

He often encourages his teams to maintain a sense of personal fulfillment alongside their professional achievements, knowing that this balance fosters long-term success both for individuals and the company as a whole. As the heir to one of the most powerful families in luxury, Alexandre Arnault is no stranger to public attention. However, he has managed to maintain a relatively private and controlled public persona. Unlike other high-profile figures in the luxury sector, Alexandre tends to avoid unnecessary media exposure, preferring to let his work speak for itself.

His social media presence, while curated, offers a glimpse into his life and interests. He shares occasional updates on his professional achievements, personal milestones, and the brands he oversees, but he remains cautious about divulging too much personal information. This careful balance between visibility and privacy has helped him maintain an air of mystery, which is fitting for someone in his position. Overall, Alexandre Arnault's personal life and experiences reflect the values he holds dear—hard work, family, creativity, and social responsibility. These qualities not only shape his approach to business but also define his character as a leader in the luxury industry.

Chapter 5: Legacy

Alexandre Arnault's journey in the luxury industry, particularly within the context of LVMH, reflects his multifaceted approach to leadership and innovation. LVMH, the world's largest luxury conglomerate, has seen unprecedented growth and diversification under the guidance of his father, Bernard Arnault.

Yet, Alexandre has played a critical role in ensuring that the group remains agile and relevant in the modern era, particularly with his pivotal work at Tiffany & Co., Rimowa, and his broader contributions to the LVMH group. Alexandre's most significant legacy is likely tied to his work in modernizing Tiffany & Co., but his contributions span far beyond that. At Rimowa, he demonstrated his capacity for reshaping iconic brands. His leadership transformed the German luggage brand into a highly sought-after luxury label, primarily through strategic collaborations with fashion designers and influencers, helping Rimowa shift from a utilitarian brand into a trendy fashion accessory.

His role in LVMH's digital transformation cannot be overlooked either; Alexandre has championed the use of technology and digital marketing to cater to younger, tech-savvy consumers who have become the key demographic in the luxury market. The luxury sector, which once relied heavily on traditional marketing methods, has been rapidly changing in recent years, with younger consumers demanding a more personalized and digital approach.

Alexandre has been a driving force in this shift, understanding the importance of engaging luxury customers online, something many legacy luxury brands were slow to adopt. Through his digital-first mindset, he has ensured that LVMH's brands stay competitive in a highly evolving market, emphasizing e-commerce, social media engagement, and influencer partnerships. His ability to leverage technology and culture to reshape a brand's image has marked him as one of the more forward-thinking executives within LVMH.

Shaping the Future of Luxury

In many ways, Alexandre's legacy extends beyond his individual achievements and contributions. He is part of a broader shift in the luxury industry, where younger generations are beginning to have a more prominent influence. As the son of Bernard Arnault, Alexandre is set to play a key role in the future of LVMH. His potential as a future CEO of the conglomerate has been widely discussed, and his legacy is closely tied to the direction the company will take under his leadership.

Alexandre represents a more modern and progressive view of luxury—one that embraces inclusivity, sustainability, and a digital-first mindset while maintaining the high standards of craftsmanship and exclusivity that have long defined the industry. His leadership at LVMH marks a significant shift toward an industry that values more than just opulence. Alexandre has embraced the idea that luxury can be both responsible and innovative. His advocacy for sustainability in fashion and jewelry is not merely a corporate strategy but an integral part of his personal ethos.

Sustainability has become a cornerstone of his legacy, particularly with his efforts to ensure that Tiffany & Co.'s diamonds are responsibly sourced and that LVMH's operations have a more minimal environmental impact. Alexandre's embrace of these practices aligns with a larger global movement toward ethical and sustainable production in luxury goods, something he has continually pushed within his role at LVMH.

In addition, his innovative approach to luxury retail—where experiences and consumer engagement take precedence over product exclusivity—has begun to reshape how luxury brands engage with their clientele. Alexandre's impact is felt not only through his direct contributions to LVMH's growth but also through the wider shifts he has inspired within the industry itself. His influence is visible in the growing number of luxury brands focusing on digital marketing, collaborating with influencers, and tapping into broader, more diverse consumer bases.

Alexandre Arnault is widely seen as a potential future leader of LVMH, the crown jewel of the luxury industry, which has been under the stewardship of his father, Bernard Arnault, since its founding. While Bernard Arnault has yet to step down from his role as the company's chairman and CEO, Alexandre is already being groomed to take the helm one day. As one of the most influential young figures in luxury, Alexandre's leadership potential has been recognized both within LVMH and throughout the broader business world.

The transition of leadership at LVMH will not be an easy one, especially given Bernard Arnault's remarkable success and near-dominance in the global luxury market. However, Alexandre is uniquely positioned to inherit the reins. His experience in various roles within LVMH, such as his tenure at Rimowa and Tiffany, have equipped him with the skills necessary to lead the group into the future. Moreover, his understanding of digitalization, global markets, and evolving consumer behavior makes him a fitting successor for LVMH, which has continuously maintained its position as the world leader in luxury through innovation and adaptation.

Alexandre's future leadership role within LVMH could involve further expanding the company's reach into emerging markets, increasing its digital presence, and continuing to lead the charge on sustainability in the luxury industry. As he gains more experience and influence, Alexandre will likely have a hand in shaping LVMH's long-term strategy, ensuring that the group maintains its market leadership while evolving with changing consumer demands.

One of the most significant challenges Alexandre will face is navigating the changing landscape of luxury. With younger generations increasingly prioritizing ethics, transparency, and sustainability, he will need to continue balancing tradition with innovation, ensuring that LVMH's prestigious heritage remains intact while embracing the future. Given his track record, Alexandre is well-positioned to rise to the occasion and carry forward his father's legacy while carving out his own distinctive imprint on the luxury industry. Alexandre's legacy is already one of innovation. His influence is evident not only in the revitalization of brands such as Rimowa and Tiffany but also in his ability to foster a culture of creative disruption within LVMH.

He has demonstrated that luxury doesn't have to be synonymous with stagnation; it can be dynamic, evolving, and inclusive. The success of his campaigns and the rebranding efforts at Tiffany and Rimowa show that Alexandre is a visionary who understands the pulse of modern luxury consumers. Moreover, Alexandre's commitment to fostering innovation isn't limited to just consumer-facing efforts; it extends to LVMH's internal workings as well.

His leadership style has been marked by a focus on technology and operational efficiency, positioning LVMH as not just a luxury powerhouse but also a company that understands the future of business. As the luxury market continues to evolve, Alexandre's legacy will be one of ushering in a new era of luxury—one that combines high-tech with high-touch, craftsmanship with creativity, and exclusivity with accessibility. Alexandre Arnault's legacy is still being written, but it is already clear that he will play a pivotal role in the future of the luxury industry. His contributions to brands like Tiffany & Co. and Rimowa have been transformative, and his forward-thinking leadership has set him apart as a key figure in shaping the luxury sector's future.

As he continues to push boundaries and innovate, Alexandre's legacy will likely be one of bringing a new level of accessibility, sustainability, and inclusivity to luxury, while still maintaining the craftsmanship and exclusivity that define the industry. His legacy, tied to LVMH, will resonate far beyond the traditional confines of luxury and into the next generation of consumers, leaders, and creators.

Chapter 6: Net Worth

Alexandre Arnault's net worth is a subject of significant interest, as he is part of one of the wealthiest families in the world. While precise details about his financial standing are not readily available due to the private nature of his wealth, it is clear that his wealth is primarily tied to his family's holdings in LVMH and his key roles within various luxury brands, especially Tiffany & Co.

His financial status is likely substantial, with some estimates suggesting his wealth could be in the hundreds of millions, if not more, considering his family's vast fortune. The Arnault family, with Bernard Arnault at its helm, has been at the forefront of the luxury industry for decades. LVMH, the conglomerate that controls some of the most prestigious brands in fashion, cosmetics, and retail, continues to expand its empire. As an executive vice president of Tiffany & Co., Alexandre holds a senior position within one of LVMH's flagship companies. Given the high valuation of Tiffany & Co. and Alexandre's direct involvement in revitalizing the brand, it's reasonable to assume that his personal wealth has seen significant growth in recent years.

Beyond his direct involvement with Tiffany & Co. and Rimowa, Alexandre's stake in LVMH's overall portfolio of brands further contributes to his financial status. LVMH's assets include renowned names like Louis Vuitton, Christian Dior, Fendi, and Moët Hennessy, among others. As a member of the Arnault family, Alexandre's financial status is undoubtedly closely linked to the performance of LVMH as a whole.

With the luxury goods market showing consistent growth, Alexandre's wealth is expected to grow accordingly, making him one of the wealthiest figures in the luxury industry. While Alexandre's precise net worth may not be disclosed, it is evident that his wealth is not only substantial but will continue to increase as LVMH continues to expand globally, and as his role within the company evolves. Alexandre's position as a key player in one of the most influential luxury conglomerates in the world places him in a unique position, and his financial standing is a reflection of his family's legacy as well as his own professional accomplishments.

Influence of Family Wealth

It is impossible to discuss Alexandre Arnault's net worth without acknowledging the tremendous influence of his family's wealth. As the son of Bernard Arnault, one of the richest men in the world, Alexandre's financial standing is intricately tied to the extraordinary success of his father's vision for LVMH.

The Arnault family's fortune is estimated to be in the tens of billions, with the vast majority of this wealth being derived from LVMH's massive holdings in the luxury goods sector. The Arnault family's wealth is not only a product of Bernard Arnault's leadership but also a result of strategic acquisitions, visionary branding, and the family's ability to steer the company through changing market dynamics. Alexandre, as the son of Bernard, benefits from this immense family wealth, which provides him with both opportunities and responsibilities. While Alexandre is highly successful in his own right, his financial status is undeniably influenced by the position he holds within the Arnault family's legacy.

However, it is important to note that Alexandre has never appeared to rely solely on this privilege. His work in transforming Rimowa and his role in rejuvenating Tiffany & Co. speak to his drive and ambition, independent of his family's wealth. That said, his access to wealth and resources has undeniably provided him with unique opportunities that many others in his industry do not have. The fact that Alexandre works within LVMH, the luxury conglomerate founded by his father, also positions him within an ecosystem where success is rewarded with substantial financial returns.

As a result, Alexandre's financial worth is not simply a product of his family's fortune but also a reflection of his contribution to the ongoing success of the brands under LVMH's umbrella. The influence of family wealth is also evident in the strategic decisions Alexandre makes within his professional life. The resources at his disposal have enabled him to make bold moves in the industry, whether it be his acquisition of Rimowa or his efforts in rebranding Tiffany & Co. Alexandre's ability to shape the future of iconic brands while being financially supported by his family's wealth creates a dynamic where he is both a beneficiary of his family's legacy and a significant contributor to its continued success.

Furthermore, Alexandre's family wealth also allows him to take risks in the business world—something that could be far more challenging without access to the financial backing that LVMH provides. This freedom allows him to experiment with new business strategies and models, positioning him as a progressive leader in the luxury industry.

Financial Independence and Personal Investments

While Alexandre's wealth is significantly influenced by his family's assets, he has also taken steps to establish his own financial independence. His work as the CEO of Rimowa was a key example of his ability to lead a luxury brand to greater success. Under his guidance, Rimowa's revenue grew significantly, and the brand's collaborations with designers like Virgil Abloh and Supreme helped it reach a new generation of consumers. These successful ventures have likely contributed to Alexandre's personal wealth, establishing him as a highly capable executive in his own right. Additionally, Alexandre's involvement in Tiffany & Co. has further cemented his financial status.

As part of LVMH's acquisition of the brand, Alexandre has had a direct hand in Tiffany's resurgence. With Tiffany's sales and brand value increasing under his leadership, Alexandre has contributed to a profitable venture that will undoubtedly have financial benefits for him, both as an executive and as a member of the Arnault family. Beyond his direct roles within LVMH, Alexandre has also made personal investments, though these are typically more discreet.

His ventures are likely to involve a mix of personal and family assets, as his position within the Arnault family's wealth structure provides him with the resources to explore new opportunities and secure his financial future. It is also possible that Alexandre has stakes in other luxury or tech ventures, as his interests span beyond traditional luxury goods. His passion for technology and digital marketing might also translate into investments in tech startups or other businesses in the digital sphere, sectors where he has demonstrated significant expertise. Despite his impressive financial backing, Alexandre has made it clear that he values autonomy and independence in his professional life.

His strategic decisions in the business world reflect his desire to build a legacy based on his own merits, not solely on his family's wealth. As is common among many billionaires, Alexandre Arnault's wealth is also a source of philanthropy and charitable work. While he is not as publicly active in philanthropy as his father Bernard, there is evidence that Alexandre participates in charitable endeavors through both his work and personal initiatives.

LVMH, under Bernard Arnault's leadership, has supported various causes related to the arts, education, and sustainability, and it is likely that Alexandre is involved in these efforts as well. Tiffany & Co., under Alexandre's leadership, has placed a stronger emphasis on sustainability, social responsibility, and ethical sourcing. These initiatives align with broader philanthropic efforts within LVMH to promote environmental and social causes. Alexandre's leadership at Tiffany also includes efforts to increase diversity and inclusivity, further solidifying his commitment to making a positive impact beyond just business.

While Alexandre's wealth is undeniably vast, it is important to recognize that he also shares in the responsibility of ensuring that it is used for good. The Arnault family's commitment to giving back, whether through direct charitable donations or through corporate social responsibility initiatives, is likely to continue shaping Alexandre's financial legacy in the years to come. Alexandre Arnault's net worth is closely tied to both his family's wealth and his own professional accomplishments.

His involvement in LVMH's brands, particularly Tiffany & Co. and Rimowa, has ensured his financial success, but his personal drive and vision have played a significant role in building his financial standing. Alexandre's wealth will likely continue to grow as LVMH expands, and his leadership within the company positions him to not only inherit his family's fortune but also build a legacy of his own. While his wealth may have been bolstered by his family's assets, Alexandre has consistently demonstrated that he is more than just the beneficiary of his father's success. His contributions to the luxury sector, combined with his entrepreneurial mindset, ensure that Alexandre's financial future remains bright and that he will continue to shape the future of luxury for generations to come.

Conclusion

Alexandre Arnault's life and career provide a remarkable narrative of ambition, innovation, and legacy. As one of the most influential young figures in the luxury industry, his contributions to brands like Tiffany & Co. and Rimowa, as well as his work within LVMH, have established him as a visionary leader with the potential to shape the future of luxury retail.

From an early age, Alexandre was immersed in the world of luxury through his family's wealth and LVMH's global empire. However, his career has been defined by a series of achievements that go beyond mere inheritance. His leadership at Rimowa demonstrated his strategic vision for transforming established brands, taking the iconic German luggage company and positioning it as a desirable luxury brand through collaborations with prominent designers like Virgil Abloh and brands like Supreme. This marked the beginning of his legacy within the luxury sector, showing that he was more than just a successor to his father's empire. At Tiffany & Co., Alexandre's impact has been even more profound.

Upon LVMH's acquisition of the jewelry brand, Alexandre assumed a leadership role and worked tirelessly to modernize Tiffany's image, leveraging digital platforms and collaborations with celebrities like Beyoncé to reposition the brand as a contemporary, sought-after luxury name. Alexandre's push for inclusivity and sustainability has helped elevate Tiffany into a modern luxury icon, blending tradition with forward-thinking strategies.

Under his leadership, Tiffany's profitability has grown, and the brand's relevance in the luxury market has been solidified, with Alexandre playing an integral role in revitalizing its global stature. One of the defining aspects of Alexandre's achievements is his ability to balance tradition with innovation. While maintaining the core values of craftsmanship and exclusivity, he has successfully introduced new strategies to engage younger consumers, integrate digital marketing, and promote sustainability. His influence has extended to the broader luxury market, where his approach to engaging consumers through digital platforms and influencer partnerships is reshaping how luxury brands communicate with their clientele.

Beyond his corporate achievements, Alexandre's personal commitment to hard work and responsibility has defined his character. He has made it clear that his success is the result of his own efforts, not simply the privilege of being born into wealth. His leadership style, marked by innovation and a focus on modernizing legacy brands, has earned him respect as a forward-thinking executive.

Alexandre is not content with merely preserving the status quo—he is determined to lead LVMH and the luxury sector into a new era that embraces technology, sustainability, and inclusivity. Looking ahead, Alexandre Arnault's future in the luxury market seems poised for further growth and transformation. As the son of Bernard Arnault, the current chairman and CEO of LVMH, Alexandre is considered a potential successor to his father, and his future leadership of the company could mark a new era for one of the world's most powerful luxury conglomerates. With his proven track record of success, Alexandre's ability to navigate the complexities of the modern luxury market makes him an ideal candidate to guide LVMH through the next phase of its evolution.

The luxury market itself is undergoing significant changes. Younger consumers, particularly millennials and Gen Z, are driving demand for brands that are not only exclusive and high-quality but also socially responsible and sustainable. Alexandre's embrace of these values, both personally and professionally, places him at the forefront of a new era for the luxury industry. Sustainability and ethical production are no longer optional; they are key drivers of brand success.

Alexandre's work, especially with Tiffany & Co., has already demonstrated his commitment to these principles, and as the market evolves, his ability to adapt and lead will continue to define his legacy. The future of luxury will likely continue to be shaped by digital transformation, and Alexandre's digital-first approach has positioned him as a leader in this area. Luxury brands are increasingly engaging with consumers through e-commerce platforms, social media, and influencer marketing. Alexandre's understanding of these dynamics, combined with his forward-thinking leadership style, ensures that LVMH will remain competitive in a rapidly changing landscape.

Moreover, Alexandre's global perspective will be an asset as LVMH expands further into emerging markets. As luxury consumption grows in regions like Asia and the Middle East, Alexandre's experience in digital marketing and understanding of diverse consumer preferences will be invaluable in navigating these markets. His ability to merge LVMH's heritage with modern strategies will continue to set the group apart from competitors in the luxury sector.

Another key element of Alexandre's future role in the luxury market will be his ability to continue driving innovation. The demand for unique, personalized experiences, combined with a greater focus on craftsmanship and storytelling, will require leaders who can navigate both the art and science of luxury retail. Alexandre's creative approach, combined with his operational expertise, positions him to lead LVMH in a way that balances the allure of exclusivity with the desires of the modern consumer. Alexandre Arnault's journey is one of extraordinary achievement, hard work, and strategic innovation.

While he has certainly benefited from his family's wealth and legacy, he has also proven himself as a leader in his own right, shaping the future of luxury with his innovative ideas and commitment to sustainability. His contributions to LVMH, particularly at Tiffany & Co. and Rimowa, have reshaped how the luxury sector approaches branding, marketing, and consumer engagement. In the years to come, Alexandre's impact will continue to grow, both within LVMH and the broader luxury market.

His vision for a more inclusive, sustainable, and digitally-savvy luxury market will likely shape the direction of the entire industry. As he moves forward in his career, Alexandre remains a figure to watch closely, as his legacy—built on his own merits and his contributions to LVMH—positions him as one of the most influential leaders of the future in luxury. Alexandre Arnault's story is far from complete, and the coming chapters in his career will likely further cement his place as one of the most important figures in the luxury industry. His leadership, vision, and drive to innovate ensure that his legacy, both as a member of the Arnault family and as an individual, will have a lasting impact on the future of luxury.

56

www.ingramcontent.com/pod-product-compliance
Lightning Source LLC
Chambersburg PA
CBHW070940220526
45469CB00007B/2457